All Scripture references taken from the KJV of the Holy Bible, unless otherwise indicated.

Shut the Front Door, Closing Evil Portals

Dr. Marlene Miles

Freshwater Press 2025

freshwaterpress9@gmail.com

ISBN: 978-1-967860-01-2

Paperback Version

Table of Contents

Shut the Front Door
Closing Evil Portals

Freshwater

Introduction

This book is more than a transcription of the Warfare Prayer Channel prayer, *Shut the Front Door, & Evil Gates & Evil Portals*, but it does include all the prayer points of that video prayer, and more.

I usually enumerate prayer points for those who pray a few points each day and want to keep up with where they left off. But the main reason I number the prayer points is for intercessors and those who pray with others, it is easy to keep up with where you are when praying together. Those who take very late and very early prayer watches will know that sometimes you might be a little sleepy and knowing where you are when praying with another person or in a group is very useful.

This book also includes some teaching on the subject matter of portals and how to know if a portal is open against you and your life. Of note, the sequencing of this event is usually started by sin. After sin, there is transgression. After transgression there is iniquity. After iniquity a stronghold is established against the sinner and or the bloodline of that sinner. This all depends on how much time passes from sinner to stronghold. The sinner could see the stronghold in his or her lifetime or may not see it, but their children could and or their *children's* children.

The stronghold is in place, so the enemy has basically set up camp in that person's life or bloodline. So, they might as well build a road directly to that person or bloodline. Those who listen to my teachings or read my books may have heard me say, quoting Prophet Kevin

Leal, "Once sin is in the third generation of a bloodline--, *it's in there*."

By the third generation, by the time of the children's children the enemy may be fully encamped and very comfortable while he steals, kills, and destroys and makes that bloodline very uncomfortable.

I kinda bet you're the third or fourth generation of somebody, aren't you? So, there are strongholds that you must tear down from your foundation that are harassing or diminishing the progress of your bloodline. When God looks at you, yes, He sees you, but He also sees your entire bloodline.

How do I know this?

Ancestry is important to God, else why are all the *begats* in the Bible? Who a person's father is is important to God. As Cain asked, being snarky, Am I my brother's keeper?

Yes, you are.

So, the stronghold that is established could affect the entire family and the entire bloodline. One sinner can do a lot of harm, even in a family.

Now the real horror, if the devil has the right to come in and out as he pleases, might as well build a direct route to that person or that family--, a portal.

These types of activities are war strategies. Woe to those who are at ease in Zion; we are at war, believe it or not. So, the enemy builds a road directly to what or who he wants to attack, harass, control, steal from, kill or destroy. At the end of that route an exit ramp is established, a way to hop off the "interstate" and get to the location the enemy wants to reach: a portal is established.

In this warfare that you should be aware of, because there are no sin-free humans, and our fore parents may have sinned, transgressed, created or inherited iniquity, allowed strongholds against our bloodline from the enemy, and possibly either opened portals or allowed one or more portals to open. We have the authority to bind and *loose* according to the Word. We have the ability and the authority to fight. So, we must fight; so we bind and *loose*.

But strongmen need to be removed. *Spirit spouses* need to be divorced and evicted, *monitoring spirits* need to be kicked out, *familiar* and *ancestral spirits* must go, and their routes need to be damaged and uprooted, destroyed and closed so they can't just show up in your life at will. Portals need to be closed. If you want to think of a game of Whack-A-Mole--, hey, if there is a way in they will try to pop up in your life. By spiritual warfare, in authority and in the position of dominion, speak the Word and at the Name of Jesus every knee must bow.

That at the name of Jesus every knee should bow, of things in heaven, and things in earth, and things under the earth;

And that every tongue should confess that Jesus Christ is Lord, to the glory of God the Father. (Philippians 2:10-11)

How?

How are these portals opened? The previous chapter outlined spiritually how it could just happen, simply by sin, unrepented sin, repetitive sin. By the efforts of the unrepentant sinner the devil is allowed to create a stronghold and the sequela to that maybe a portal is opened against that person and or bloodline.

Sin is sin, but some sinners are more committed to sin than others. Some are more prideful, greedy, devilish--, some have opened portals on purpose. We've heard some of the supposed brilliant minds of the world say they just go open a portal, at will, to access certain information; those people are being deceived. Jesus is the Way, the Truth and the Life, if you are not accessing Jesus, then anything else is counterfeit. *Familiar spirits* can provide "information" to a seeker who is not seeking the Lord and if that person has "opened a portal," then they have just opened a portal. There is other worldly information in the second heaven, where the seat of Satan is that a man can access and be pretty impressed by. If it is not from God, then it is not true, not completely true, it is dangerous and should not be used or handled.

Maybe not today, but one day, that willful portal opener may wonder why their life is going to hell and things are not working out. This may be evident when we see the meteoric rise of a celebrity or person. We may soon see their meteoric fall. That is the nature of second heaven agreements.

The Lord, however, is slow and steady. In Christ we bear fruit, even much fruit, but fruit that remains.

It's the "portal" they opened in their deception or greed, and they have given hell free reign in their life and the lives of their bloodline, unless they accept Christ and close that portal. We may not see their meteoric fall, but we may see the torment and turmoil in the lives of their children and their *children's* children.

When conjuring up a devil or demon, the person on this side is opening up the portal. The person actually opens up and establishes the portal, believing that they want this demon to come into the Earth realm. Why would they want that? Power. Fame. Money. Revenge are the usual reasons.

And those things are sought after and people either of their own do this conjuring, or they go to someone who will do it for them. Diviners. Necromancers. Sorcerers. Witches. Warlocks, Wizards. Priests. Priestesses. Star gazers, Astrologers, Shamans, occultists, and the like.

While some purposefully open up portals to hell, some can do it accidentally or just by chance. Stop playing around with this sort of thing, and if you think your child is, you'd better teach them very well not to do this. Children playing demonic games, using Ouija boards, watching demonic shows, that you or they may not even know are demonic can open up a portal. Any repetitive, ritualistic behavior has the ability to do that. So don't let your kids stay glued to TV and devices, especially if you don't know what they are delving into or looking at.

Have you noticed that ever since your kid started watching a certain show they have nightmares every night or almost every night?

A portal is open.

Simply saying the wrong thing (especially over and over) can invite the demonic. Giving worship of any kind to the dark side can invite them. When you invite someone to your house, for example, do you not look for their arrival? Do you not get up and open the door for them and usually say something like, *"Come in."* Well, that is so much less work for the dark side to come into and invade your house and your life versus them having to try to deceive you, trick you, entice you, or lure you—but those are devil tactics and ways to get in, also.

The point is we must look to see what may be the signs that one or more evil portals are open in your life.

Saints of God, as we speak of having an open Heaven over us so that our prayers are heard and as the Lord blesses us we can actually receive those blessings. Conversely if demonic, evil, witchcraft, occultic portals are open that is the same as having an open hell beneath you. The imagery is that if hell is open below you, the devil is only waiting for a person to slip one more time.

Close those portals; don't be his victim.

Thou hast enlarged my steps under me, that my **feet** did not **slip**. (Psalm 18:36 and 2 Samuel 22;37)

But as for me, my **feet** were almost gone; my steps had well nigh **slip**ped. (Psalm 73:2)

Altars

An altar is the interface between the physical world and the spiritual world. An altar could be for good or for evil. What is invoked at that altar is what will come through.

Be wise.

Altars take or require sacrifice. There is no free lunch, and there are no free demons. You bring up a demon, it wants a sacrifice. It wants worship and or a sacrifice. If you don't give it willingly, it has ways. So don't play with this.

Be very wise. Don't even accidentally conjure up something that you either don't know what it is, what it requires, and you can't even give it even if you knew what *it* required. The fantasy imaginings of a human during sex, either with someone or masturbating alone is also conjuring. Sexual fluids have DNA. God hates spilled seed, spilled blood, and demon worship.

An altar is a place of sacrifice, by definition. Any place where blood has been shed is an altar. Evil people go to places of sacrifice and altars on purpose for the evil energy that is in that place. Portals are established in these places. You go there, you could pick up anything, anything could follow you home. Any of the places listed where people conjure up devils and demons is or has an altar. That is why if you go there, it is not what it seems to be and you will get a *familiar spirit* from then on. You visit and altar, that *spirit* believes you are now a devotee, and they want worship from you.

Disaster sites, war zones, battle sites--, any place where blood was shed. If you must go there, you'd better pray, be prayed up, and be prayerful while there. It is best that the Lord *sends* you, more so than you simply decide to go there. It would be the absolute worst thing to do is to go there against the advice of the Lord. That would be an enter at your own risk sort of thing.

But don't we realize the amount of rubbernecking that goes on in traffic, for example when an accident happens that people want to see trouble? What is this *morbid curiosity*?

I vaguely remember the story of a person who went to the shrine of an idol and slept there. What followed them home terrified them. There are many shrines across the world that allow that. People go to what they believe are "spiritual" places on purpose for what they believe will help or empower them, but really they are sleeping in places of open portals, and they get tagged by a demon or two. Tag, they are now it, and *It* follows them home. Just because a place is spiritual, doesn't mean it is of God.

A bar, for example, is a portal or usually established over a portal. That's a great place to sell *spirits* and do all the other things that happen in a bar. Whether you drink or not, if you go there, you have attended the place of an open evil portal. If God sent you, then you are okay. I think of the woman who years ago, her husband was not home late into the night, as usual. She knew he was at the bar, so she went in her church suit and hat along with a giant Bible, the kind people usually keep open in their house back in the day. She went to get her husband, to snatch him from the fire.

She was laughed out of there. Depending on whether God sent her or whether that was her bright idea will we know if she was spiritually covered to even go into a place where debauchery occurs on the regular. That raucous behavior is worship to idols and demons, devils and imps.

Don't we realize by what people seek to watch in the movies and on TV that they want to see that sort of thing? Folks, those things can open portals into your home--, whether the kids watched the show with you, or not. People who believe themselves good parents are concerned that their kids don't become frightened by what they see. Really good parents should be concerned that their kids are not frightened or hurt by what they don't see. Don't unleash hell in your house and then wonder why it is there.

Wherever there is bloodshed--, any kind of blood, that is an altar. You should pray every time you see or approach an altar. You should be prayed up and stay prayed up, especially if you happen upon a portal.

When you think about it, do we not erect monuments to dead things, dead people and places of bloodshed all too often? Why is that? Why is the world fascinated with that, and should Christians also be?

I went to the sight where the current 911 monument is, and I wish I'd never gone. Like so many, I had prayed about 911 and for the people hurt, lost, and harmed for many years. Our Midtown hotel where we usually stay, was not available the first night we arrived in NY, so we stayed at a nice, new hotel that actually overlooked this thing.

We toured the monument up close and I prayed silently thee, but it gave me the *heebie jeebies*. Its not just the names recorded on it, this thing is alive. The way the water swirls and then goes downward, now that I'm thinking about it, is as if a portal to hell was opened by 911, but instead of closing it, whomever was commissioned to make this "monument" left it open to celebrate it in some way.

That monument, that whole area interrupted my sleep. A place of sacrifice and bloodshed is an altar. Human sacrifice creates a portal. I do wish I had neither gone there, nor slept there or in the vicinity of this place. If you go, go with permission of the Lord, or be sent. Be prayed up. Don't just go as on vacation to see it as a sightseeing adventure.

We need Jesus. All day, every day. 24/7.

This Should Not Be Happening

Are things happening in your life that you know should not be happening? Do you too often end up with the short end of the stick? You know this is not right because you're supposed to be the head and not the tail. Do you look outside onto your lawn, and it looks terrible, even though you put a lot of work into it? Does your neighbor's yard look perfect, and he has a dog, and you don't?

Is this a game of opposites? His dog should not be using your yard and tearing it up, but it is. You've spoken to them, you've spoken to the dog, but neither one of them seems to understand.

24

Of course, when they think you are not home, they let the dog run free, but you are home, and you see what is happening.

The dog has free reign to come into your yard because there is no fence up. There are no barriers. There is nothing to stop that little dog. But why is the dog choosing your yard and not theirs? The neighbors moved into their house before your house was ever built so the dog used to play on the lot that is now yours. The dog has *marked* that territory and even though you live there, you have not spoken in a language that the dog understands to let it know not to come into your yard. Neither have you put up a barrier, such as a gate or a fence to stop it. The owners of the dog, well, they don't really care because their yard looks fine, so why would they care about yours?

You should not be getting the short end of the stick when you don't have and haven't invited anything into your yard that could damage it.

I'm not calling your neighbor a devil, but the devil is like that. He has certain territory that he has *marked*, and he thinks that gives him the right to come into that space whenever it suits him. He thinks that he has free reign.

How do you even know that the dog has been in your yard, if you're at work or not sitting looking out the window all day?

Well, there's evidence. The dog could leave markings, droppings, your grass is bald and dug up where the animal used your yard.

There is evidence in the spiritual realms and also in the physical realms that the devil has entered, intruded into or sneaked into your life and messed up things for you. We just have to pay attention. Getting saved may make a person think that the devil will never bother them again; that is not always true.

Shouldn't you win more, and more often? When did your dream life change to the point that you don't even want to go to sleep some nights because of the warfare you must endure every night. These are signs. When your dream life changes, God is trying to let you know that in the spirit realm, things are different.

But you're a warrior, right? So, God is teaching your hands to war? That could be true, but don't use that as sole justification that everything is alright or that you don't need to do anything other than what you are doing or what you have been doing. I have come to realize that there are things that I go through for real on the job training, and once I realize it and do something about it--, usually pray pointed and appropriate prayers, the situation usually goes away immediately.

So, battles come. If they are not fought, what could be a battle could turn into a whole war. If the enemy lays siege and establishes himself in opposition to your abundant life that you should be having, it will be much harder to unseat him than if you handled it while it was only a battle.

If the little dog was trained not to go into the empty lot before a house was there, he would never have marked the territory or established the pattern of going there. Now he is not trainable, and/or his owners do not care. In the real case of this real dog, both are probably true. In reality, that's a little dog, it could do better, but the ownness is on the ones that allow him to continue polluting their neighbor's yard. The owners empower the dog to come into their neighbor's yard because the dog can't let himself out of the house. And they further empower the dog by letting it do whatever it likes while outside. The malicious, competitive neighbor who wants their yard to be better than yours, will send his animal into your yard to ruin it.

In the case of the devil who sends little demons and devils, or worse, those annoying imps need to be sent out of your yard, out of your house, out of your life, and the ability for the enemy to send them has to be shut down, closed off.

In war, first you must know your enemy. Who are you warring against, really? What weapons are they using? Have you sized up those weapons? Have you studied them? They've certainly sized you up and they have studied you and every weapon that you have access to. They have developed or tried to develop a counter to every weapon that you have access to. They know which weapons you don't know about, and which ones you know about and don't have a clue how to use. They're laughing at that. They are laughing if you have powerful spiritual weapons that you can use against them, but you are not using them.

The enemy also knows which weapons you can use, and they are prepared in case you decide to use them.

Uh, use them, please?

Are you prepared? You don't know what time your neighbors are going to let the dog out any more than you know when the devil will send a demon to annoy or harass you. Therefore, stay prepared. Prepare more for the spiritual than worrying about the lawn and a little dog.

Spiritual enemies have been alive for millennia and are prepared. The only hope you and any of us have is to be in Christ for knowledge of their plans against mankind. Be in Christ for Wisdom on how to access that Wisdom and how to use it. Be in Christ for empowerment, anointing and the ability to do battle and war against the enemy. And, be in Christ for protection against this enemy. And we must be in Christ for the victory.

Else, how do you fight an empowered enemy who has strategies, and knows every flesh move that a man could ever make? You can't fight a spiritual opponent in the flesh, in your flesh.

Signs That A Portal Is Open Against You

- Constant battles
- Constant attacks
- Dream life is a battle or fight every night or very often.
- *Monitoring spirits* (follow-follow spirits)
- Strange happenings around you.
- You keep attracting evil or demonic people.
- You are tormented, either in the natural or in your dream life, or both.
- The things that beset or entrap the people in your bloodline are blaring in your life or in your

family's lives and you just can't seem to break free of evil cycles.

- Even if it it's only one thing: You can't seem to get breakthrough in that one area of your life, it could be that a portal to enforce that one thing against you is open.
- Such as: Poverty. Anti-marriage, barrenness, etc.
- Sudden, mysterious and unexplained losses and failures.
- *Spirit spouse* or any demon or devil that you realize is resident in your home or wherever you go.

Fear Not

The authority and the Voice to keep things that shouldn't be on your lawn, off your lawn is in your position and authority in Christ Jesus. You just have to pray to keep the enemy from sending (or allowing) what wants to come into your space, out of your space, your house, your life, your family and your bloodline. You have to pray, make decrees and declarations, in the Name of Jesus.

The LORD is my light and my salvation; whom shall I fear? the LORD is the strength of my life; of whom shall I be afraid? (Psalms 27:1)

1. Lord, if I am a sinner, save me by Your Mercy and Your Grace; make me one of yours. I believe that Jesus is the Son of God and He came to Earth and died for my sins. On the Third Day, God raised him up and He lives. Lord Jesus, Come into my heart and be the Lord of my life, in the Name of Jesus.

2. In the whole armor of God, the armor of LIGHT, I stand to pray and go to the Throne of God, in the Name of Jesus.

3. Put on the whole armour of God, that ye may be able to stand against the wiles of the devil.

    For we wrestle not against flesh and blood, but against principalities, against powers, against the rulers of the darkness of this world, against spiritual wickedness in high *places*.

    Wherefore take unto you the whole armour of God, that ye may be able to

withstand in the evil day, and having
done all, to stand.

Stand therefore, having your loins
girt about with truth, and having on
the breastplate of righteousness;
And your feet shod with the
preparation of the gospel of peace;

Above all, taking the shield of faith,
wherewith ye shall be able to quench
all the fiery darts of the wicked.
And take the helmet of salvation, and
the sword of the Spirit, which is the
word of God:

Praying always with all prayer and
supplication in the Spirit, and
watching thereunto with all
perseverance and supplication for all
saints; (Ephesians 6:11-18)

4. Lord, cover me with the Blood of
Jesus.

5. The Blood of Jesus. The Blood of
Jesus.

6. HOLY GHOST FIRE, fall and help me in these prayers, in the Name of Jesus.

Sin, Transgression, Iniquity, Stronghold, Portal

7. Sin – every sin of divination, bloodshed, adultery, fornication, witchcraft, robbery: I renounce the sin, I denounce it. LORD, I ask for Your forgiveness and Mercy. Wash me with the Blood and by the washing of the Water of the Word, in the Name of Jesus.

8. Every transgression of rebellion, idolatry, bitterness, injustice, impurity, immorality, greed, Lord, forgive, cover me with the Blood of Jesus.

9. Father, change my filthy rags into a proper garment to be in Your Presence. Lord, do not turn Your face away from me, in the Name of Jesus.

10. Iniquity of sin, whether old sin or new sin--, whether the iniquity of the sins of my ancestors, parents, or me, Lord blot out our transgressions and remove the iniquity so that the devil will have nothing in us, in the Name of Jesus.

11. Strongholds – every familial, generational, and ancestral stronghold be removed, be torn down. Let the evil covenants that uphold you be canceled, demolished, burned to ashes with Holy Ghost Fire, in the Name of Jesus.

12. Lord, deliver me from temptation, in the Name of Jesus. (X3)

13. Lord, deliver me from the sins that so easily beset me and those in my bloodline, in the Name of Jesus.

14. Lord, deliver us from the sins that so easily beset us, in the Name of Jesus.

15. Lord, I break, cancel and dismantle the ungodly and evil things that our family is likely to do, and the covenants that put those things in place. Things that are just in our nature, things that are in our sin nature, I renounce those things, I denounce them. Things that are in our foundation and our bloodline, that we are just likely to do--, Lord, help us. Deliver us from temptation deliver us from sins and transgressions and evil.

16. Lord, purge our bloodline with the Blood of Jesus. Amen

Portals

What is a portal? The meaning of portal is *door, entrance*; especially a grand or imposing one. It can be akin to or described as a door or a gate. In languages such as Spanish, a door is, *puerte*. In French it is *porte*. See how close the words are.

I picture the beginnings of a demonic portal to be something like a sinkhole. When it opens to the other side, then it is a portal. It is a conduit, a channel or a tunnel from one place to another place.

If you consider ley lines to be invisible but spiritually known *spiritual* pathways or roads that lead from one place to another, then once you get to that place how do you get into that place. Now, put on your thinking cap because the issue is that the different places are different realms. Therefore someone (or something) could leave a place, take a journey to get out of that place and when they get to where they are going, it is another whole realm, with its own atmosphere so how do they get into it? How do you get into any place.

A door? A gate? A portal?

If there is security or guards or other obstacles or requirements or restrictions to getting into another whole realm, how would one get in?

If a group of people walk from one country to another country and there is border patrol at the border, then they have to get in legally or find another way in. A demonic portal is not the legal way in.

Jesus said, I stand at the door and knock.

Behold, I stand at the door, and knock: if any man hear my voice, and open the door, I will come in to him, and will sup with him, and he with me. (Revelations 3:20)

Jesus says you get in by knocking. That is, if you are not a thief, usually you just go up to the front door and knock.

The devil may stand at the door and while he is knocking, he's probably sent a bunch of devils around to the side and the windows and anyplace else to figure out a way in.

Verily, verily, I say unto you, He that entereth not by the door into the sheepfold, but climbeth up some other way, the same is a thief and a robber.

But he that entereth in by the door is the shepherd of the sheep.

To him the porter openeth; and the sheep hear his voice: and he calleth his own sheep by name, and leadeth them out.

And when he putteth forth his own sheep, he goeth before them, and the sheep follow him: for they know his voice.

And a stranger will they not follow, but will flee from him: for they know not the voice of strangers. (John 10:1-5)

A demonic portal is not legal, it is hidden and supposed to be a secret, most likely. That portal is not the legal door but that does not mean that an evil human agent didn't authorize it either knowingly or unknowingly, on purpose or accidentally. There are many spiritual things that cannot happen in the Earth unless a human agrees with it. As before stated, there are many types of evil human agents, whether they realize they are or not. Whether they think they are, or not.

If you are one who can see in the spirit, you may become aware of such. If you hear the Holy Spirit, and you are prayerful, He may just tell you. Or, if you wait long enough and enough stuff happens to you, you may start to put A & B together and figure out that something just isn't right in your life. Then after researching, reading the Word, teaching, you may realize that one or more evil portals may have been opened, maybe over millennia by your ancestors and the devil figured out a direct route to the people in your bloodline. All the while you may be guarding the front door and very proud that you've shut that door, locked it and even have an alarm on it---, in the natural.

Except the Lord watch, they that watch, watch in vain.

It would behoove any and all of us that if Jesus is standing at the door, that we let Him in so when it comes to guarding and watching the city, we have spiritual help. In our flesh we are no match for what the devil can bring. We need spiritual

Help and the Help the Lord brings is superior to anything that could come against us. Not only that, we cannot *see* unless the Lord gives us *eyes to see.*

> But blessed *are* your eyes, for they see: and your ears, for they hear. (Matthew 13:16)

Ever see a lawn with mole hills? Those are portals through which the little animals travel undetected underground and then they come up when they are ready. They make a mess of a lawn and kill the grass. Without spiritual vision you won't see a portal. Without hearing in the Spirit, you won't hear about it when the Holy Spirit gives a Word of Knowledge. If you think your life is great and if you're going through something, you say it's just life, then you may never look deeper than surface. You may never figure out if a portal is opened, or what type of portal is against your bloodline.

Foremost, without the Lord you will not be empowered to close it.

And to the angel of the church in
Philadelphia write; These things saith he
that is holy, he that is true, he that hath
the key of David, he that openeth, and
no man shutteth; and shutteth, and no
man openeth;

I know thy works: behold, I have set
before thee an open door, and no man
can shut it: for thou hast a little
strength, and hast kept my word, and
hast not denied my name. (Revelations
3:7-8)

Look closely at the conditions
required in the above verse. First realize
in the flesh, there is little strength. The
Word even says that the spirit is willing,
but the flesh is weak.

Finally, my brethren, be strong in the
Lord, and in the power of his might.
(Ephesians 6:10)

We must keep the Word of the
Lord and not deny His Name. Therefore,
if we are in Christ, and all in and don't
flake out or vacillate, then we can also in
Christ, handle doors, gates, and portals.
Verse 7 mentions the Key of David: if you

have the key to a place, you either own it or you have the authority to enter into that place. You have the ability to close it and lock it. You have the Grace to let others in, and the empowerment to lock others out. David worshipped the Lord and was a man after God's own heart. Worship lets a man into the presence of the Lord. In your proper authority and dominion, given by God, by salvation and relationship, you are authorized.

David is a lineage. Jesus Christ is called the Son of David. We are in Christ, therefore we are also *in David*. By inheritance you get what your ancestor or father had. Therefore, you too, may be given a key. In Christ and in the presence, there is power and there is ability and authority to shut doors (portals) and with the key, keep them closed against you and your family.

It would be appropriate to seal closed portals by the Holy Spirit and or with the Blood of Jesus. Amen.

So, in the Beginning after God had created the Heavens and the Earth and said, It is good, if the Earth was void and without form, had the devil turned the whole thing into a *portal*? Nowhere in the Bible does it say that the Heavens were void and without form. It was only Earth that had that description.

If you had or built a fine car, I the natural and it required petrol to run, but you hooked it up to a hose that delivered sugar water, wouldn't the whole thing be ruined? You could take something good and ruin it by what it is hooked up to, what it is connected to.

So, could it be that our warfare is realizing, among other things, that portals are open and close them, close them, close them? Doing so would lock those who are beneath our feet in their own realms, even in their own tunnels or conduits and keep them from coming into the Earth realm. And after so doing, connect the Earth back to God, back to what and how it was originally intended to be *hooked up*?

See how what Christians do is diametrically opposed to what evil human agents do? They invite these entities and beg them to come, while those of us who are in Christ should be breaking up evil altars, tearing down evil gates, and closing evil *portals*.

17. Every evil portal that is against me and my bloodline, shut that door, in the Name of Jesus.

18. Lord, every evil portal that is open against me or my bloodline, I ask that You shut the door, and seal it, in the Name of Jesus.

19. Every evil portal that is against me and my bloodline, shut it please Lord, in the Name of Jesus.

20. Every affliction that I have noticed or not noticed-

21. Every affliction that I have felt or not yet felt--,

22. Every affliction that that I've experienced or not even been aware that I've experienced --,

23. Whether I've seen these afflictions or whether they are hidden–,

24. Whether they have happened, or whether they are waiting for an appointed time, a season, a day or an hour–, Lord, break that assignment over me and my family, in the Name of Jesus.

25. Lord, heal every affliction by Your Word. Lord, just send the Word and heal me, heal us, heal my family and bloodline, in the Name of Jesus.

26. Lord, Heal us of all confusion, brain fog, madness, insanity, foolishness.

27. Lord, heal us of all barrenness of every kind, poverty, insufficiency, and lack, in the Name of Jesus.

28. Lord, heal us of infirmities, save us from death and heal us from all addictions, in the Name of Jesus.

29. Heal us and remove all shame, reproach, oppression, blindness, rejection, demonic possession; deliver us Lord, in the Name of Jesus.

30. Father, heal us of violence in our family line. Heal us from abuse, and

sorrow, and every kind of defilement, in the Name of Jesus.

31. Lord, Remove every judgment in the Name of Jesus by Your lovingkindness, and Your Mercy.

32. Lord, we beg Mercy. we ask for Mercy, Lord. Mercy, Lord Jesus, in the Name of Jesus.

33. We pray for Mercy.

34. Son of David, have Mercy on us.

35. Every portal, gate, every door I close you by the power in the Blood of Jesus, the King of Kings; He is the Lord.

36. I close doors that no man can open again in my family line, in the Name of Jesus.

37. Every affliction--, new or chronic that is in my life, or that is the result of an open portal against me, be closed by the Power in the Blood of Yeshua.

38. My family name--, every spiritual door to fornication, lying, stealing, adultery, disrespect of mother or father, or of men, or women, that is associated with my name, my surname or family name, whether I married into that name or I was given it at birth, I declare by the power in the Blood of Jesus that that portal is hereby closed and never again to reopened by the Word and the power of the Lord. Amen.

39. Father, let that door, that gate – that portal that afflicts me in any way, be closed hermetically and permanently, in the Name of Jesus.

40. Let the LORD: post a Mighty angel with a flaming sword that turns every

which way to keep out every evil spiritual entity, *spirit*, devil or demon, or evil human agent, in the Name of Jesus.

41. Every portal of desperation, or lack, insufficiency or poverty is hereby closed, never to be reopened by any evil agent or entity, in the Name of Jesus.

42. Every portal to idolatry and *whoredoms* of any kind, for any reason opened by anyone in my bloodline, be closed today, right now, and permanently shut, in the Name of Jesus.

43. Every portal to witchcraft of any kind, from any source, opened by anyone in my bloodline, for any reason, be closed permanently, today, by the power in the Blood of Jesus.

44. I shut every witchcraft portal in my foundation, in my bloodline, in my family line, or caused even by me, in the Name of Jesus.

45. Lord, forgive. Lord, forgive me, in the Name of Jesus.

46. Lord, remove the iniquity, in the Name of Jesus.

47. Every portal of sexual perversion of any kind, allowed in my bloodline by anyone at any time, for any reason, whether they did it knowingly or unknowingly, willingly or whether they were forced, I close that door, (X3). I close that gate, and that portal, NOW, in the Name of Jesus.

48. Every portal of unjust balance, be closed, in the Name of Jesus.

49. Every portal of insufficiency and lack, be closed, in the Name of Jesus.

50. Every portal of occultism, mysticism, witchcraft, or any dark arts, be closed, in the Name of Jesus.

51. Every evil portal of health problems, health concerns, illness, disease, disorder, syndromes, or symptoms of ill health that had been opened by anyone in my bloodline, be closed now, now--, never to open again over this bloodline, in the Name of Jesus.

My Blood

52. I SPEAK TO MY BLOOD--,
I SPEAK TO MY BLOOD.
I SPEAK TO MY BLOOD and MY
BLOODLINE: BE HEALED. BE
HEALED. BE MADE WHOLE of
every dread disease, disorder,
inherited negative trait, every
syndrome, every symptom, or any
terminal disease in the Name of Jesus.

53. Be healed. Be healed.

54. I speak to my blood, I speak to my
cells, I speak to the tissues of my body,
I speak to every organ, and I say: BE
HEALED. BE HEALED, be made

whole of every dread disease, disorder, inherited negative trait, every syndrome, every symptom, or any terminal disease in the Name of Jesus.

55. BE HEALED, Now.

56. NOW, GOD is--, BE HEALED NOW.

57. I dismiss you--, every disorder and disease: I dismiss you from my blood and my bloodline. I send every enforcing demon, devil, or entity back to wherever they came from, back to whoever sent them.

58. I go back in time to when this disease first came into my bloodline or family line. I now, by the power in the CHRIST OF GOD, in the Name of Jesus, I close the portal by which you come in and out of my life and the lives of my family members, in the Name of Jesus.

59. I close it by the power in the Christ of God, Amen.

60. Every evil portal – every person in my family line who is an evil human agent knowingly, or unknowingly, every evil portal that allows or invites or has invited evil into my family bloodline, the LORD Jesus Christ rebuke you and shut you off from the evil power that you are accessing, in the Name of Jesus.

61. Every walking, talking, evil portal, lose my address, lose my location – forget my name and stay away from me, and mine, in the Name of Jesus.

62. Jesus is my Gate: I am in Christ and therefore I have no association, no alliance, no relationship with you, in the Name of Jesus.

63. I am in Christ. I am in Christ. I am in Christ.

Evil Altars, Evil Humans

64. Every evil altar, every strange altar in my family bloodline, I tear you down, I break you with the Thunder Hammer of God. Be discomfited and dismantled with power lightnings from the armory of the LORD and never regather again, in the Name of Jesus.

65. Every evil human agent in my family bloodline I commend you into the hands of the Lord God, and if you insist on being evil and doing evil, the LORD put a sword between me and you. Lord, put a wall of fire between me and you, and between you and the

rest of our bloodline that is serving the LORD GOD, Jehovah God, in the Name of Jesus.

66. Every evil portal that is affecting me or my life, be shut down against me, by the power in the Blood of Christ.

67. LORD, I forgive whoever sinned, transgressed, or brought this iniquity into my bloodline whether they did it knowingly or unknowingly, but I reject the portal they opened to me and my family, I reject it. I reject that portal. I reject it, and I refuse to leave it open.

68. LORD, close the doors that no man can open again, in the Name of Jesus. (X2)

69. Lord, close every evil door, every evil gate, and every evil portal that no man can open it against me again, or

against my family again, in the Name
of Jesus.

70. Every portal that the Thief has opened
to steal from my family, by the power
in the Blood of Jesus, and by the
Winds of God, I shut that access point
and seal it forever, in the Name of
Jesus. (X2)

71. Any evil, demonic, occultic,
witchcraft portals opened over my
home or my dwelling place, by the
power in the Name of the Christ of
God, I close them forever, in the Name
of Jesus. (X3)

72. Any evil, demonic, occultic,
witchcraft portals opened over my
office, business, or workplace, by the
power in the Name of the Christ of
God, I close them forever, in the Name
of Jesus. (X2)

73. Any evil, demonic, occultic, witchcraft portals opened over my school or wherever I study, be closed by the power in the Blood of Jesus. Amen.

74. Any evil, demonic, occultic, or witchcraft portals opened over me, or affecting my life or the lives of anyone I know in a negative or evil way, CLOSE, CLOSE, CLOSE, and be shut by the power of God, by the power of the Most High, and let no man ever open them again, in the Name of Jesus.

75. Any evil demonic, occultic, or witchcraft portal opened over my ministry, my spiritual gifts, or anything that the Lord has assigned for me to do as my purpose and to reach my destiny, be shut, shut, shut, forever, in the Name of Jesus.

76. I bind every evil interference over my life, my marriage, my children my family, my career, my business, my finances, my health, my purpose and my destiny, in the Name of Jesus.

77. Thief, you have been discovered: return all of what you have stolen from me and my bloodline since you have been stealing from us, in the Name of Jesus.

78. Since you've been stealing from us, from the time you first started, return everything sevenfold back to me and our bloodline, in the Name of Jesus.

79. I am in Christ we are in Christ.

80. I am in Christ; We are in Christ.

81. Every sin, transgression, iniquity, stronghold, or portal of **anger** over me or my family, I reject anger, I reject

you, I renounce you, I denounce you, in the Name of Jesus.

82. Father, close every portal of the stronghold of **anger** over me and my family, in the Name of Jesus.

83. Every sin, I renounce you, I denounce you, in the Name of Jesus.

84. Every sin, every portal of sin, I renounce you, I denounce the sin, and Lord, I ask You to close that portal. In agreement, I close it by the power in the Blood of Jesus. Amen.

85. Every iniquity, be blotted out with the Blood of Jesus; I am the righteousness of God, in Christ Jesus.

86. Every stronghold and strongman, be bound and removed from this evil gate, this evil access point. Lord, send Your mighty angels to bind and

remove every strongman at every evil gate, so that gate can be closed, sealed and removed from my life, forever, in the Name of Jesus. Amen.

87. Enemy attacks, enemy oppression, enemy challenges, enemy assaults, cease. You will bow at the Name of Jesus. Every knee shall bow at the Name above all names, things in Heaven and Earth and beneath the Earth, in the Name of Jesus.

88. That at the name of Jesus every knee should bow, of things in heaven, and things in earth, and things under the earth;

And that every tongue should confess that Jesus Christ is Lord, to the glory of God the Father. (Philippians 2:10-1)

89. Every portal of the works of flesh – every portal opened and that remains open over me and my family, you must be shut today, now, in the Name of Jesus.

Every Evil Portal

90. Every portal of unforgiveness that may easily beset my family, I close you by the power in the Blood of Jesus.

91. Every portal of greed, I close you, in the Name of Jesus.

92. Every portal of resentment and bitterness, I close you, in the Name of Jesus.

93. Every portal of selfishness, I close you, in the Name of Jesus.

94. Any portal that disrespects mother or father, or any that break any of the

commandments of GOD, I close you
by the power in the Blood of Jesus.

95. Every portal of murmuring and
complaining, I close you by the power
in the Blood of Jesus.

96. Every portal of rage, I close you by the
power in the Blood of Jesus.

97. Every portal of revenge, I close you by
the power in the Blood of Jesus.

98. Every portal of gluttony, I close you
by the power in the Blood of Jesus.

99. Every portal of lust, I close you by the
power in the Blood of Jesus.

100. Every portal of idol worship, I
close you by the power in the Blood of
Jesus.

101. Every portal of idolatry, I close you by the power in the Blood of Jesus.

102. Every portal of *Whoredoms*, I close you by the power in the Blood of Jesus.

103. Every portal that is coming against me or my family, I close you, in the Name of Jesus.

104. Every portal of false Christ worship, I close you, in the Name of Jesus.

105. Every portal of false religions, I close you, in the Name of Jesus.

106. Every portal of *error*, I close you, in the Name of Jesus.

107. Every portal of serving Mammon, I close you, in the Name of Jesus.

108. Every portal of alcoholism or drug abuse, I close you by the power in the Blood of Jesus.

109. Every portal of addiction of any kind, I close you by the Power in the Blood of Jesus.

110. Every portal of witchcraft to include gambling, to include lottery, raffles and all games of chance, which are all Lorded over by the evil marine kingdom, I slam the door in your face, you no longer have access to move in and out of my family as you may have had, the LORD JESUS rebuke you.

111. We are in Christ, and you are dismissed by the power in Christ. We are saved now, we are in Christ, in the Name of Jesus.

112. Every portal of lying and cheating which we may have opened which

now has flipped the script and working against us, LORD we repent, Lord, forgive and remove the entities enforcing losses in our lives, and shut the door, shut the door, close the door, close the portal, in the Name of Jesus.

113. Lord, please close all portals of evil judgments against us, in the Name of Jesus.

114. Any portal that has been allowed in my bloodline through parents, ancestors, Lord, let that portal close and every evil dimensional access point to my life, let it be shut and sealed by the Blood of Jesus.

Shut the Front Door

115. Lord, forgive me for any portal that I have allowed to be opened against me, my life, or my family, in the Name of Jesus. (X2)

116. Lord, forgive me for any portals that I opened or that I allowed to be opened, even on my **watch**, by my ignorance, by my rebellion, by my negligence, foolishness, laziness, in the Name of Jesus. Lord, forgive.

117. Except the Lord watch the city, they that watch, watch in vain.

118. Except the Lord build the house, they labour in vain that build it: except the LORD keep the city, the

watchman waketh *but* in vain. (Psalm 127:1)

119.   Lord, I am a city; Lord, forgive me for not watching this city when I should have been watching.

120.   Lord, forgive me for not watching correctly or watching only in my flesh, or thinking I could do it without You: Lord, I need You 24/7.

121.   So, even in the whole armor of God I watch, I watch and pray – I watch, I watch & pray.

122.   Father, forgive me for only shutting the front door to the obvious and ignoring the other potential access points, or living carelessly, not paying proper spiritual attention, in the Name of Jesus.

123.   Lord, forgive me when I didn't snatch that family member of my own family--, snatch them from the fire, not realizing that they were potentially opening evil doors, not just for themselves, but opening evil doors and access points and maybe enabling a portal to be opened by the enemies of God to that they could come into our bloodline.

124.   Lord, forgive me for not doing proper ministry if I have failed You, and others, in the Name of Jesus.

125.   Lord, forgive me for not dealing with relatives and friends who were not only opening access points, or portals, but themselves may have been evil portals and wherever they went, it rained evil in some way, shape or form.

126.   Lord, forgive me. Lord, help us. Lord, help me.

127.   Lord, deliver me from all evil that I have allowed in my own house, knowingly or unknowingly, especially any that could have either been a walking demonic portal or a portal that was opened in my house or my business without me being aware of it, in the Name of Jesus.

128.   Lord, help me. Deliver me from all evil that I have allowed in my own house, knowingly or unknowingly, especially any that could have been a walking demonic portal or an agent who could have opened a portal in my house or over my house or business without me being aware of it, in the Name of Jesus. (X2)

The Blood of Jesus

129. We need you Lord, 24/7. Deliver us Lord, in the Name of Jesus. I plead the Blood of Jesus. The Blood of Jesus. The Blood of Jesus. Lord, cover me, in the Name of Jesus.

130. Holy Ghost Fire, make my dwelling place, my workplace, my school and even me too hot for the enemy to stand, and let them fall, in the Name of Jesus.

131. I plead the Blood of Jesus.

132.   The Blood of Jesus. The Blood of Jesus. Lord, I plead the Blood of Jesus cover me.

133.   Lord, if I am in darkness in anyway, bring me out, call me out, take me out of captivity and bring me fully into Your marvelous Light, in the Name of Jesus. (x2)

I Am the City

134. The ones that were planning that the city be their caldron – I AM the city, and I am not their cauldron, in the Name of Jesus.

135. I am not their candidate, I am not their sacrifice, I am not their cauldron, I am not their victim, in the Name of Jesus.

136. Lord, shut the door, the gate, the portal against them that give them access to this City, or the other people in my bloodline, in the Name of Jesus.

Forced Portals

PORTALS THAT WERE FORCED OPEN IN OUR BLOODLINE:

137. Portals of slavery: I am not your slave, I am not your slave, I am not your slave. I do not work for free. I do not work for free. I do not work for nothing and no pay, in the Name of Jesus.

138. I am in Christ.

139. I am a bondservant of Christ. I do not work for the world for free. I am in Christ.

140.   The workman is worthy of his hire. I study to show myself approved, I am a worthy workman, in the Name of Jesus.

141.   Pharoah, I am not your slave (X3), in the Name of Jesus.

142.   You are not my master – any portal that is opened to pharaoh and any pharaoh-like *spirits* or entities who want the fruit of my labor, let that portal be closed, let it be closed, let it be closed., in the Name of Jesus.

143.   Let it trap them forever in their own hell, until the Judgement, in the Name of Jesus.

144.   Jesus is the Lord of my life, I do not need and do not accept any other *lords* in the Name of Jesus.

145. Jesus is the Lord of my life, I do not need and do not accept any other *lords*, just Jesus, He is the Lord of my life, in the Name of Jesus.

146. All portals of maliciousness and evil, I close you, in the Name of Jesus.

147. Portals of negligence, laziness, desolation, hopelessness, depression, be **CLOSED** and sealed against me and mine, in the Name of Jesus.

148. Portals of home insecurity, I close you, in the Name of Jesus. (X2)

149. Portals of repeated losses, and repeated thefts and burglary and robbery, I close you, in the Name of Jesus.

150. Every portal of food insecurity, I close you, in the Name of Jesus.

151. Every portal of housing insecurity, I close you, in the Name of Jesus.

152. Every portal of *familiar spirits,* I close you, in the Name of Jesus.

153. Every portal of ancestral *spirits,* I close you, in the Name of Jesus.

154. Every portal of *monitoring spirits,* I close you, in the Name of Jesus.

155. Every portal of enforcing demons, demons sent to enforce curses, I close you, in the Name of Jesus.

156. .Every portal of night terrors, I close you, in the Name of Jesus.

157. Every portal of nightmares, I close you, in the Name of Jesus.

158. Every portal of dream affliction of any kind, I close you, in the Name of Jesus.

159. .Every portal of dream masquerade and other spiritual trickery, I close you, in the Name of Jesus.

160. Every portal of *spirit spouse,* I close you, in the Name of Jesus.

161. .Every portal of *spirit children,* I close you, in the Name of Jesus.

162. .Every portal of astral projection, I close you, in the Name of Jesus.

163. .Every portal of deception, *error,* foolish choices and wrong choices against me or my bloodline, be closed permanently, in the Name of Jesus.

164. Lord, grant us Wisdom and the Mind of Christ for right thinking, right decisions, Wise choices and the sharing of wise counsel, in the Name of Jesus.

Prayers for Discernment

165.   Lord, give us ears to hear, in the Name of Jesus.

166.   Lord, give us eyes to see, in the Name of Jesus.

167.   Lord sharpen our spiritual discernment; fill us again with fresh Anointing by Your Holy Spirit, in the Name of Jesus.

168.   Lord, give us understanding so that in all of our *getting* we get Understanding, in the Name of Jesus.

169. Every portal of jesting, mischief, and sin—every portal of the wasting of time, I close that portal now against my life and against the lives of my family, in the Name of Jesus.

170. Portals of violence, physical attacks and beatings, rape, homicide, suicide, be closed against me and my family, forever, in the Name of Jesus.

171. Portals opened in my life or my bloodline promoting headache, chronic headache, migraine or any maladies of the head, brain, nervous system, any other part of the body, be closed against us, in the Name of Jesus.

172. Portals opened in my life or my bloodline promoting diabetes, cancer of any kind and any other dread, chronic, or terminal disease, be closed, by the Blood of Jesus. By His

stripes—by the stripes of Jesus Christ we were healed. Amen.

173.   Portals opened in my life or my bloodline that bring musculo-skeletal problems into my body, every muscle, or joint disorder, let that portal that brings pain of any kind into my life, or into the lives of my family members, be shut against me against us, be shut against me and against us forever, and sealed by the Blood of Jesus.

174.   Portals opened against my life or my bloodline for premature aging, or untimely death—I cancel that assignment, I cancel it. I cancel that assignment, and Lord close that portal by the power in the Blood of Jesus and seal it against my bloodline, forever, in the Name of Jesus.

175.   Portals opened against me or my bloodline for incidents, accidents and

trauma, be closed now and forever, in the Name of Jesus.

176.   Evil portals against my marriage and the marriages of the people in my bloodline, be shut forever, in the Name of Jesus.

177.   Evil portals against happy and successful marriage and the marriages in my bloodline, be shut forever, in the Name of Jesus.

178.   Evil portals against productive and fruitful marriages, and the marriages in my family bloodline, close and remain closed against us and be sealed shut by the Blood of Jesus.

179.   Portals against education in our bloodline that hinder, block, or stop education, be closed against us, in the Name of Jesus.

180.   Portals that steal educational and other certificates and diplomas or

renders them useless, be closed against me and my bloodline, forever, in the Name of Jesus.

181. Open evil portals for thieving demons, devils and idols, be shut and sealed against us, in the Name of Jesus. And return everything you stole sevenfold, in the Name of Jesus.

182. Evil portals that block salvation and the hearing of the Word of God, in my family and bloodline, be slammed shut today, in the Name of Jesus.

Let There Be Light

183. Every portal, every a dark hole, every black hole that is granting access to darkness into my life --, into any aspect of my life, or into the lives of my spouse, my children, my family, my business or ministry, be closed, in the Name of Jesus.

184. Light has no communion with darkness. (X2)

185. Just as the Lord said, Let there be Light. I make the same decree:
186. Let there be Light. In my life, over my life, over me and in me, over my

house, my ministry, my business, in the Name of Jesus.

187.   I call for the Light of Jesus Christ. Jesus, The Light of the World.

188.   Thy word is a lamp unto my feet, and a light unto my path. (Psalm 119:105)

189.   Lord: Let me walk in Light, let me walk in the Light of Jesus Christ, the light of Wisdom, the Light of Understanding, and Truth.

190.   Then Jesus said unto them, Yet a little while is the light with you. Walk while ye have the light, lest darkness come upon you: for he that walketh in darkness knoweth not whither he goeth. (John 12:35)

191.   Then spake Jesus again unto them, saying, I am the light of the world: he that followeth me shall not walk in darkness, but shall have the light of life. (John 8:12)

188. And the light shineth in

darkness; and the darkness
comprehended it not. (John 1:5)

189. Lord, let me comprehend, let me
understand, let me discern and
perceive, Jesus the Light of the World
and shun all darkness, in the Name of
Jesus.

190. Lord, let me shun all works of
darkness in the Name of Jesus.

191. Let me walk as a child of the Light.

192. For ye were sometimes darkness,
but now are ye light in the Lord:
walk as children of light: (Ephesians
5:8)

197. But if we walk in the light, as
he is in the light, we have
fellowship one with another, and
the blood of Jesus Christ his Son
cleanseth us from all sin. (1 John
1:7)

193. Let your light so shine before
men, that they may see your good

works, and glorify your Father
which is in heaven. (Matthew 5:16)

This then is the message which we
have heard of him, and declare
unto you, that God is light, and in
him is no darkness at all. (1 John 1:5)

194.   There is no shadow of turning in
the Lord.

195. But ye are a chosen generation, a
royal priesthood, an holy nation, a
peculiar people; that ye should
shew forth the praises of him who
hath called you out of darkness into
his marvellous light: (1 Peter 2:9)

200. And I will bring the blind by a
way that they knew not; I will lead
them in paths that they have not
known: I will make darkness light
before them, and crooked things
straight. These things will I do unto
them, and not forsake them. (Isaiah
42:16)

196.   Lord, make darkness Light, make
any darkness around me, near me,

or coming toward me Light, in the Name of Jesus.

197.　The light of the body is the eye: therefore when thine eye is single, thy whole body also is full of light; but when thine eye is evil, thy body also is full of darkness. (Luke 11:34)

198. Make me FULL of light, in the Name of Jesus, let no evil be in me, let evil have no affiliation or attachment nor opportunity with me, in the Name of Jesus.

199. The people which sat in darkness saw great light; and to them which sat in the region and shadow of death light is sprung up. (Matthew 4:16)

204. As long as I am in the world, I am the light of the world. (John 8:5)

200. Lord, all the wrong places I've been, wash me by the Blood of Jesus and the washing of the water by the Word. Wash me clean of spiritual defilement

and pollution from all the wrong places that I went knowingly or unknowingly, willingly, by deception, or by force, in the Name of Jesus.

201. Lord, let Your Light flood over me, in me, and through me to cleanse me of all darkness picked up along the way or from wrong and evil altars, evil portals, and places I've been, in the Name of Jesus.

202. Lord, wash me clean of wrong things I have seen and watched on TV and in movies that have polluted my soul. Lord, restore my soul, in the Name of Jesus.

Gates of Hell

And I say also unto thee, That thou art
Peter, and upon this rock I will build my
church; and the gates of hell shall not
prevail against it. (Matthew 16:17-18)

Upon the revelation that Jesus is
the Christ of God, the gates of hell shall
not prevail against those who are HIS
Church, His called out ones.

Wide is the gate that leads to destruction.
Narrow is the way that leads to the
Kingdom of Heaven and few there be that
find it. Lord, let me find it. Let me walk in
the right way, upright before you, in the
Name of Jesus.

Jacob saw Angels ascending and
descending upon the Earth via what we

now call Jacob's ladder. Portals from Earth to Heaven exist, at the site of Godly altars.

Portals from hell to Earth also exist at the sites of evil altars.

203. Her steps go down to hell. Witches, and occultists opening up evil portals of hell, unleashing hell, authorizing hell to work in the Earth. Lord forgive, in the Name of Jesus.

204. But her end is bitter as wormwood, sharp as a twoedged sword.
205. Her feet go down to death; her steps take hold on hell. (Proverbs 5:4-5)

206. Lord, Close every evil portal against my life, in the Name of Jesus. No matter who opened it or when, in the Name of Jesus.(2)

207. LORD forgive all iniquity in my bloodline as I repent for my parents, and my ancestors all the way back to Adam & Eve, in the Name of Jesus.

208. Lord, crush every ladder the enemy uses to gain access to my life, in the Name of Jesus.

209. For God, who commanded the light to shine out of darkness, hath shined in our hearts, to give the light of the knowledge of the glory of God in the face of Jesus Christ. (2 Corinthians 4:6)

210. Lord, command the Light to shine in my darkness, over my darkness. (x3)

211. Lord, chase the darkness away from me. give me the Light of the Knowledge of the Glory of God, in Jesus Christ, Amen.

212. Thank You, Lord for hearing prayers and answering, in the Name of Jesus.

Seal These Prayers

213. I seal these words, prayers, decrees, declarations across every dimension, realm, era, timeline, past, present and future to infinity. I seal them with the Blood of Jesus and the Holy Spirit of Promise.

214. Every retaliation against these words, prayers, decrees, declarations, or against the speaker, the listener or anyone who prays these prayers at any time in the future, let that retaliation backfire with reverb against the evil perpetrator to infinity, without Mercy, in the Name of Jesus Christ. Amen.

Just as God told Gideon to tear down those evil altars that his father had erected and then build new, Godly altars, we have to close evil portals before we can open Heavenly portals. Else, God will not pour out from Heaven to have it slide right down into hell.

If you were filling your sink with water, would you turn on the faucet before you secured the stopper in the sink? Without the stopper the drain is a portal for all the water that is flowing from above to drain into or be captured. Next, we will work on having an open Heaven over us now that hellish portals are closed. **Amen**.

Dear Reader

The Lord deals with us all in unique ways. But by word of testimony, I will tell you that it was the night after I prayed these prayers, not the night I prayed them because that night I didn't go to bed until somewhere between the Third or the Fourth Watch, so I wasn't asleep long enough to dream. But the following period of sleep the Lord showed me two old suitcases at the bottom on my stairs packed and tied up and ready to go. Whatever had been oppressing me and my house had to go, Hallelujah!!!

So, stay prayerful and faithful; the Lord will deliver. Amen.

Shalom,

Dr. Marlene Miles

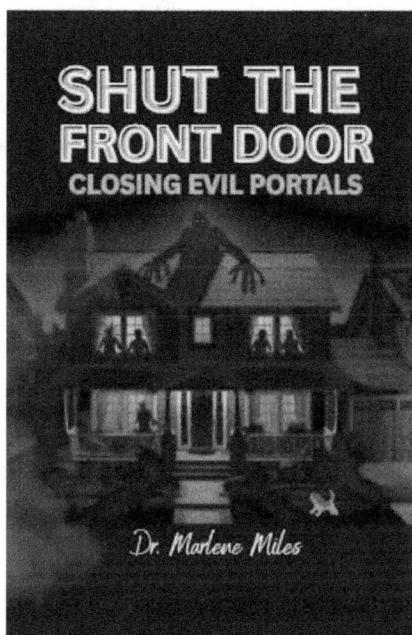

Thank you for acquiring and reading
this book and supporting this ministry.
This prayer is on Warfare Prayer
Channel:
https://www.youtube.com/watch?v=I-
tkldNw0BU

Prayerbooks by this author

While most books by this author have prayer points either throughout the book or at the end, there are some books that are only prayers. You just open up the book and pray. They are listed below:

Prayers Against Barrenness: *For Success in Business and Life*

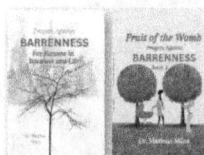

Fruit of the Womb: *Prayers Against Barrenness*

Beauty Curses, *Warfare Prayers Against*
https://a.co/d/5Xlc20M

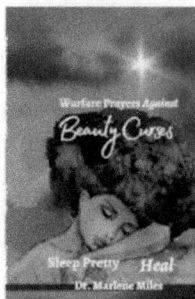

Courts of Marriage: Prayers for Marriage in the Courts of Heaven

(prayerbook) https://a.co/d/cNAdgAq

Courtroom Warfare @ Midnight

(prayerbook) https://a.co/d/5fc7Qdp

Demonic Cobwebs *(prayerbook)*

https://a.co/d/fp9Oa2H

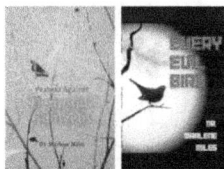

Every Evil Bird https://a.co/d/hF1kh1O

Gates of Thanksgiving

Spirits of Death, Hell & the Grave, Pass Over Me and My House

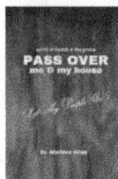

Throne of Grace: Courtroom Prayer

Warfare Prayer Against Poverty
https://a.co/d/bZ61lYu

Other books by this author

AK: The Adventures of the Agape Kid

Already Married in the Spirit: *Why You May Not Be Married in the Natural*

AMONG SOME THIEVES

Ancestral Powers

Anti-Marriage, *The Spirit of*

Backstabbers https://a.co/d/gi8iBxf

Barrenness, *Prayers Against*
https://a.co/d/feUltIs

Battlefield of Marriage, *The*

Beware of the Dog: Prayers Against Dogs in the Dream.

Bless Your Food: *Let the Dining Table be Undefiled*

Blindsided: *Has the Old Man Bewitched You?* https://a.co/d/5O2fLLR

Break Free from Collective Captivity

Broken Spirits & Dry Bones

By Means of a Whorish Father

Casting Down Imaginations

Churchzilla, The Wanna-Be, Supposed-to-be Bride of Christ

Demonic Cobwebs (prayerbook)

Demonic Time Bombs

Demons Hate Questions

Devil Loves Trauma, *The*

Devil Weapons: Unforgiveness, Bitterness,…

The Devourers: Thieves of Darkness 2

Do Not Swear by the Moon

Don't Refuse Me, Lord (4 book series)
https://a.co/d/idP34LG

Dream Defilement

The Emptiers: *Thieves of Darkness, 1*
https://a.co/d/5I4n5mc

Evil Touch

Failed Assignment

Fantasy Spirit Spouse
https://a.co/d/hW7oYbX

FAT Demons (The): *Breaking Demonic Curses* https://a.co/d/4kP8wV1

The Fold (5-book series)

- The Fold (Book 1)
- Name Your Seed (Book 2)
- The Poor Attitudes of Money (3)
- Do Not Orphan Your Seed (4)
- For the Sake of the Gospel (5)
- My Sowing Journal

Gang Ups: Touch Not God's Anointed

Getting Rid of Evil Spiritual Food

https://a.co/d/i2L3WYQ

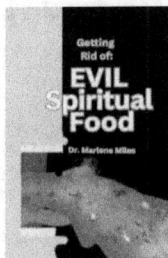

got HEALING? Verses for Life

got LOVE? Verses for Life

got HOPE? Verses for Life

got money? https://a.co/d/g2av41N

Here Come the Horns: *Skilled to Destroy*
https://a.co/d/cZiNnkP

Hidden Sins: Hidden Iniquity

https://a.co/d/4MthOwa

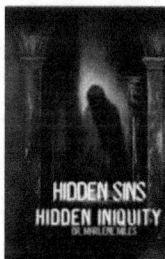

How to Dental Assist

How to Dental Assist2: Be Productive,
Not Wasteful

How to STOP Being a Blind Witch or
Warlock

I Take It Back

Legacy

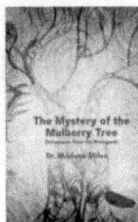

Motherboard (The) - *Soul Prosperity Series*

Name Your Seed

Occupy: *Until I Return*

Plantation Souls

Players Gonna Play

Portals: Shut the Front Door: Prayers to Close Evil Portals.

Power Money: Nine Times the Tithe

https://a.co/d/gRt41gy

The Power of Wealth *(forthcoming)*

Powers Above

The Robe, Part 1, The Lessons of Joseph

The Robe, Part II, The Lessons of Joseph

Seasons of Grief

Seasons of Waiting

Seasons of War

Second Marriage, Third--, *Any Marriage*

https://a.co/d/6m6GN4N

Seducing Spirits: Idolatry &
Whoredoms

https://a.co/d/4Jq4WEs

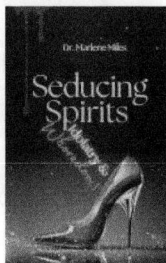

Sexual Intimacy Prayers for Married
Couples

Shut the Front Door: *Prayers to Close
Portals*

Sift You Like Wheat

Six Men Short: What Has Happened to
all the Men?

Soul Prosperity soul prosperity series 3

https://a.co/d/5p8YvCN

Souls Captivity soul prosperity series 2

The Spirit of Anti-Marriage

The Spirit of Poverty

StarStruck

SUNBLOCK

The Swallowers: *Thieves of Darkness*, 3

Take It Back

This Is NOT That: How to Keep
Demons from Coming at You

Time Is of the Essence

Too Many Wives: *Why You Have Lady
Problems*

Tormenting Spirits
https://a.co/d/dAogEJf

Toxic Souls

Triangular Power *(series)*

- Powers Above
- SUNBLOCK
- Do Not Swear by the Moon
- STARSTRUCK

Unbreak My Heart: *Don't Let Me Die*

Uncontested Doom

Unguarded Hours, *The*

Unseen Life, *The* (forthcoming)

Upgrade: How to Get Out of Survival Mode

- Toxic Souls (Book 2 of series)
- Legacy (Book 3 of series)

The Wasters: *Thieves of Darkness,* Bk 2
https://a.co/d/bUvI9Jo

What Have You to Declare? What Do You Have With You from Where You've Been?

When I Was A Child, *I Prayed As a Child*

When the Devourer is Rebuked

https://a.co/d/1HVv8oq

The Wilderness Romance *(series)* This series is about conducting a Godly relationship and marriage with someone who is a Wilderness person. It is about how to recognize it and navigate through it. These books are about how not to get caught up in such.

- *The Social Wilderness*
- *The Sexual Wilderness*

- *The Spiritual Wilderness*

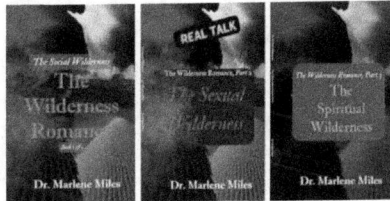

Other Series

The Fold (a series on Godly finances)
https://a.co/d/4hz3unj

Soul   Prosperity   Series
https://a.co/d/bz2M42q

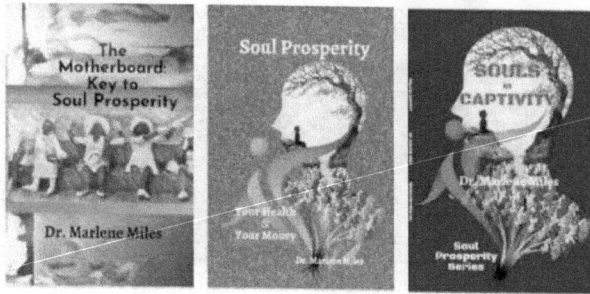

Spirit Spouse books

https://a.co/d/9VehDSo

https://a.co/d/97sKOwm

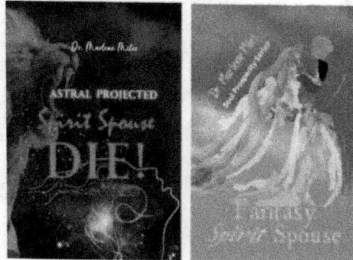

Battlefield of Marriage, The

https://a.co/d/eUDzizO

Players Gonna Play

https://a.co/d/2hzGw3N

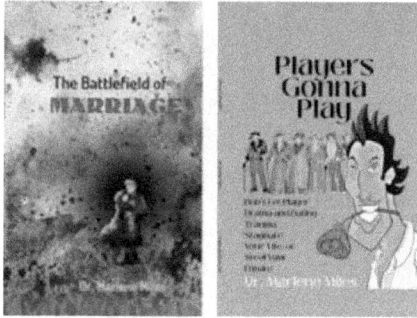

Sent Spirit Spouse (can someone send you a spirit spouse? This book is not yet released.)

Sent Spirit Spouse (forthcoming)

Matters of the Heart

Made Perfect in Love
https://a.co/d/70MQW3O

Love Breaks Your Heart
https://a.co/d/4KvuQLZ

Unbreak My Heart
https://a.co/d/84ceZ6M

Broken Spirits & Dry Bones
https://a.co/d/e6iedNP

Thieves of Darkness series

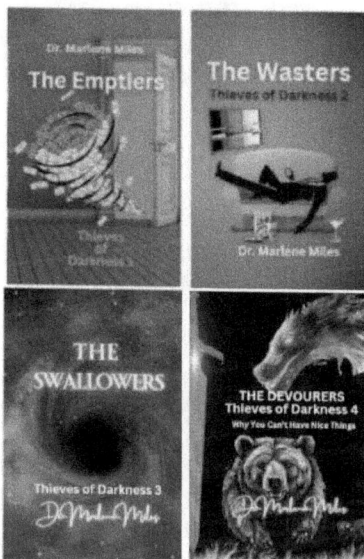

The Emptiers https://a.co/d/heio0dO

The Wasters https://a.co/d/5TG1iNQ

The Swallowers
https://a.co/d/1jWhM6G

The Devourers: Why We Can't Have Nice
Things https://a.co/d/87Tejbf

Triangular Powers https://a.co/d/aUCjAWC

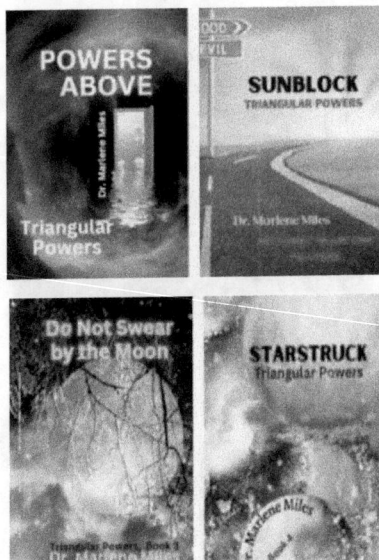

Upgrade (series) *How to Get Out of Survival Mode* https://a.co/d/aTERhX0

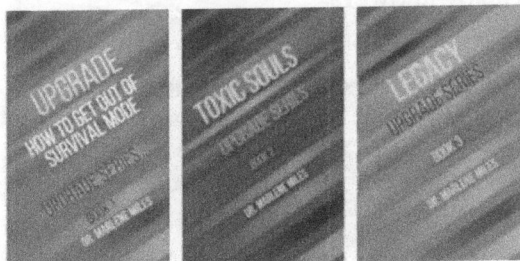

www.ingramcontent.com/pod-product-compliance
Lightning Source LLC
LaVergne TN
LVHW052032080426
835513LV00018B/2291